NanaTech

A Tech Teenager Shares Essential Skills
for Getting the Most Out of Your iPhone

By Spencer Humes

T0019608

Copyright © 2023 by Spencer Humes

All rights reserved.

No portion of this book may be reproduced in any form without written permission from the publisher or author, except as permitted by U.S. copyright law.

"NanaTech: A Tech Teenager Shares Essential Skills for Getting the Most Out of Your iPhone" is an independent (publication) and has not been authorized, sponsored, or otherwise approved by Apple Inc.

While every precaution has been taken in the preparation of this book, the publisher and author assume no responsibility for errors or omissions, or damages resulting from the use of the information contained herein.

First edition 2023.

ISBN: 979-8-35092-719-1

For Nana Gail and Granna Nola

CONTENTS

WHAT IS THIS GUIDE

Modern technology changes really fast. Anyone who regularly uses any smartphone or computer could immediately tell you many stories about times when functions changed or they opened their computer to find everything looked totally different. This can be frustrating, but we can work around it by learning the 'why' of each computer Skill. This guide aims to build a computer Skills dictionary of interconnected ideas that build on each other. Learning to use a smartphone or computer in this way is a lot like learning to drive. Most cars have totally different steering wheel layouts, they might have a different number of gears, and be vastly different in size. Even so, knowing how to drive makes it easy to drive a different vehicle because one knows the 'why' behind each action they take.

HOW THIS GUIDE IS STRUCTURED

Each chapter of this guide teaches one Skill. As new Skills are introduced, they reference previous Skills. This is helpful because modern smartphones and computers are structured in the same way, with a core set of ideas informing the design and interface of more complicated features. As you move through this guide, you'll encounter comparisons between the way things work on a smartphone or computer and a system or action that exists in the real world. These comparisons are not just intended to help build a 'why' based understanding; they also often offer a look at how design decisions are made by technology designers..

A NOTE ON DESIGN

Practically every function of a modern smartphone or computer is inspired by something in the real world. From desktop interfaces to the invisible code that makes everything work, everything is designed to mimic existing structures. This means that anyone can use a smartphone or computer with a high level of skill by using what they already know to inform how they use a device. For example, someone who's comfortable with the Dewey Decimal System would feel right at home in any settings app once they're able to see how similar the two systems are. This guide aims to illuminate those similarities.

ORIENTATION

Learning the physical features of your iPhone is an important step in becoming comfortable with this helpful device. Clockwise from the top of your iPhone they are: the handset speaker, power button, charging port, handset microphone, volume adjustment buttons, and ringer switch. You'll also notice cameras on the top and back of your phone. Your iPhone also has a dark gray oval on the right side and an oval with a dot in it on the left side. These are an antenna and SIM card reader, both are parts of how your phone accesses cellular networks, but aren't buttons or sensors we use to operate the device.

The buttons on your iPhone–the power button on the right and the volume buttons on the left–have a short travel; they don't move very much when pushed. They can feel like pushing an elevator button. The volume buttons control how loud your iPhone's speakers are if you're watching a movie or listening to music on your phone. The top button makes the speakers louder and the bottom button makes them quieter. Above the volume buttons, is the ringer switch. This switch controls the sounds your phone makes when receiving calls or other notifications. When the switch is towards the back of the phone, and the slim red line is visible behind it, the phone will not ring or chime. This can be helpful in situations where you don't want to be interrupted by your phone, such as in a theater or while you are sleeping.

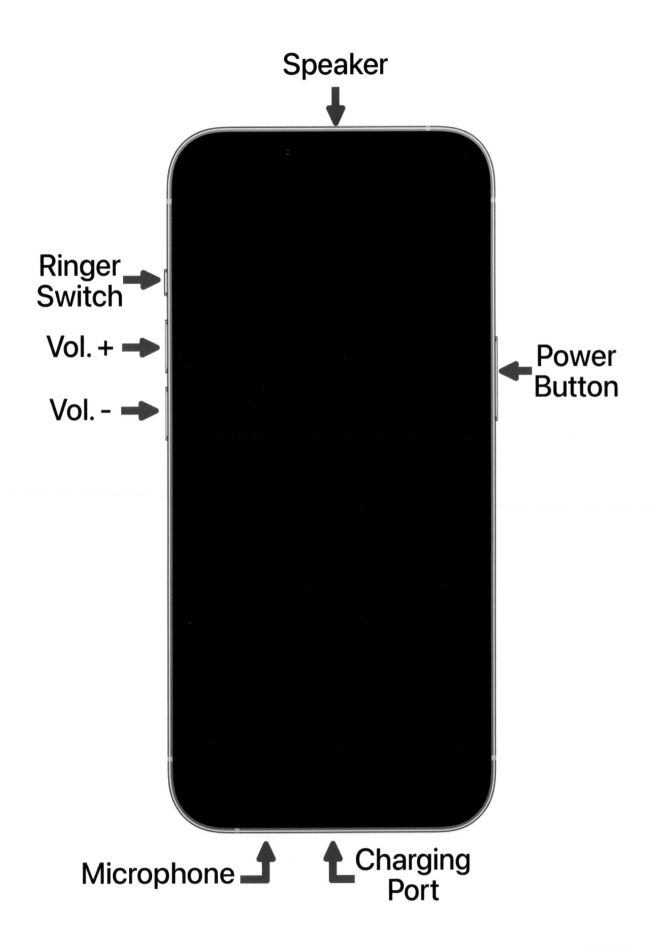

Speaker

Ringer
Switch

Vol. +

Vol. -

Power
Button

Microphone

Charging
Port

SKILL 1 **How to turn your phone on**

Many modern phones are able to tell when they're picked up, and turn on automatically. However, this feature does not always work so it is important to understand how to turn your phone on without relying on its sensors.

STEP 1. Make sure your phone is right side up.

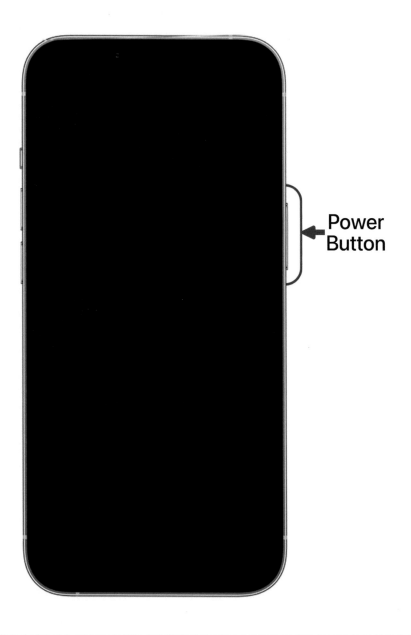

Power Button

STEP 2. Now that your phone is laid out properly, find the power button and push it once firmly and briefly to illuminate your phone screen.

STEP 3. If your phone is not unlocked, you'll see the date and time written in the middle near the top of the screen. Use the pad of your thumb to quickly swipe up from the bottom of your screen. Imagine you're sliding a playing card across your phone screen.

REMEMBER
It's important to push both physical buttons and buttons on the screen with confidence.

STEP 4. Once you've swiped up on your screen, you should see a number pad on your screen. This is where you can enter your phone's passcode. Press each number as if you were checking if bread dough has risen. It's okay to enter your password incorrectly. If this happens many times in a row, your phone may require you to wait five minutes before trying again. This can sometimes happen in your pocket or bag. If it does, don't worry everything on your phone is safe and you'll be able to access it soon. If you forget your password, you will require a professional to assist you. I would recommend reaching out to whomever manufactured the phone and speaking with them. Be cautious of anyone online or in your email who claims to be able to unlock your phone.

STEP 5. Once your phone is unlocked, it will open to what you were doing when you last used your phone. To return to your homescreen, swipe up from the bottom of the screen like you did when preparing to enter your password.

STEP 6. Now that you've reached your homescreen, you're ready to use your phone. The home screen is like the table of contents for your phone. It doesn't perform any functions by itself, but helps you choose what to do next.

You're now ready to move on to learn Skill 2

SKILL 2 How to turn your phone off

STEP 1. Find the button you used to turn your phone on.

STEP 2. Push the button firmly and briefly. Your screen should turn off. If you were listening to music or watching something on your phone, it is possible that the audio could continue to play. To avoid this, pause any audio or video before turning your phone off.

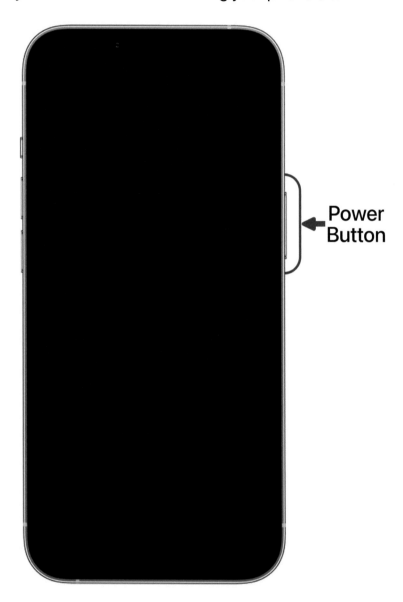

Power Button

You're now ready to move on to learn Skill 3

 To unlock your phone, use the pad of your thumb to quickly swipe up from the bottom of your screen. Imagine you're sliding a playing card across your phone screen.

SKILL 3 **How to make the text bigger**

Modern phones have many features that make them better and easier to use. My favorite of these increases the size of text almost everywhere on the phone.

STEP 1. Unlock your phone and reach the homescreen as in Skill 1.

STEP 2. Find the "**Settings**" app.

STEP 3. Open the "**Settings**" app by pushing on its icon firmly and briefly.

The "Settings" app controls many different functions on your phone. Each one of the icons you see in the list opens a menu of different functions related to it. Rows of these icons are sorted into related blocks separated by an empty line.

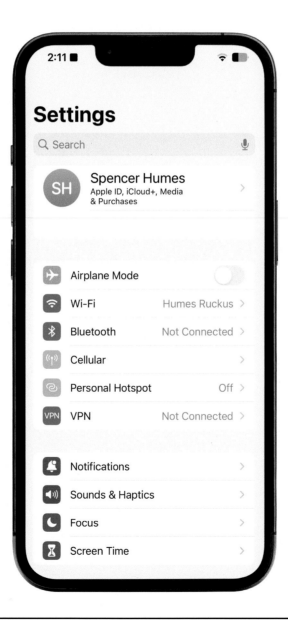

STEP 4. Using the pad of whichever finger is most comfortable for you, slowly swipe up your screen. The list should move upwards. Imagine that the list is a sheet of paper you're sliding along the surface of your phone. **You're looking for the row titled "Accessibility."** It should be in the third block of rows.

STEP 5. Press firmly and briefly on any part of the "**Accessibility**" row. You should see a new list of options appear. **The first one should read "VoiceOver."** All of these functions are useful to help you see, hear, and interact with anything on your phone.

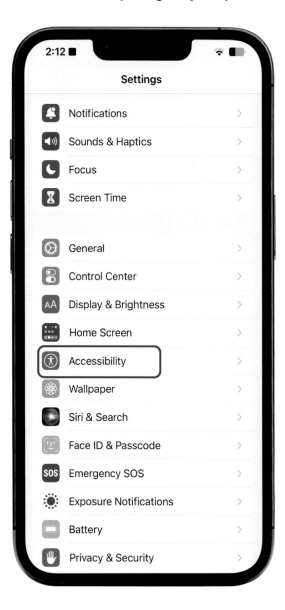

STEP 6. Press firmly and briefly on the row titled "**Display & Text Size.**"

STEP 7. The second item in the new list you just opened should say "**Larger Text**." Press on it firmly and briefly.

At the top of the screen you should see a box which says "**Larger Accessibility Sizes**" with an oval with a dot in it. At the bottom of the screen you should find a gray line with a white dot in the middle. (see next page)

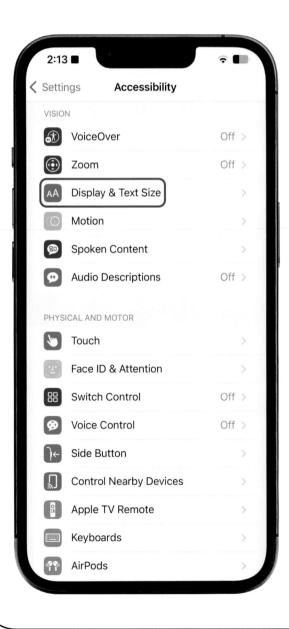

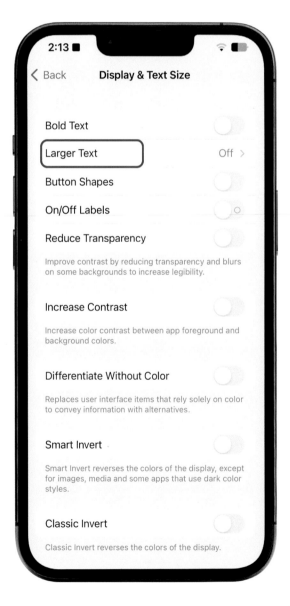

STEP 8. Using the pad of your finger, press on the white dot on the line and slide it to the right. Imagine that it is a small circle of paper you are sliding across your phone.

STEP 9. You should see the text under the first line become larger. **Slide the white dot on the bottom of the screen until it reaches a comfortable size**. If you have moved the dot all the way to the right, and the text is too small, press firmly and briefly on the white dot in the upper right size of the screen. The oval it is in should turn green and the white dot on the gray line on the bottom of the screen should move

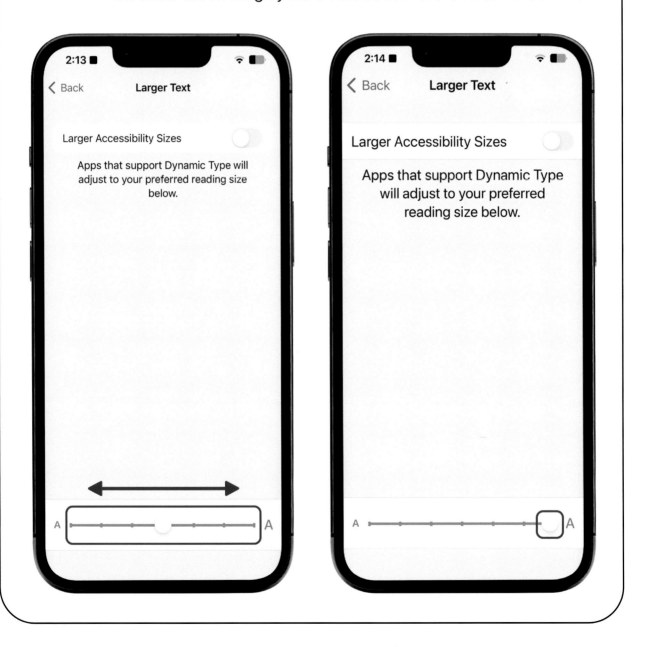

to the left. You may now make the text much larger. If the largest size available is not comfortable, I'd recommend selecting a smaller size of text combined with reading glasses or a reading magnifying glass.

STEP 10. Once you're happy with the text size you've selected, press firmly and briefly on the blue arrow titled "**Back**" in the upper left hand corner of your screen.

STEP 11. Feel free to select any other options from the "**Display & Text Size**" menu by pressing on the white dots next to the name. My favorites are "**Bold Text,**" "**Increase Contrast,**" and "**Reduce Transparency.**"

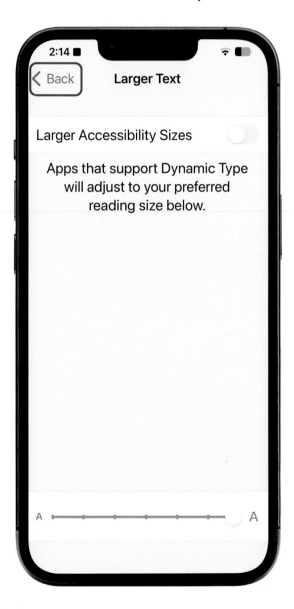

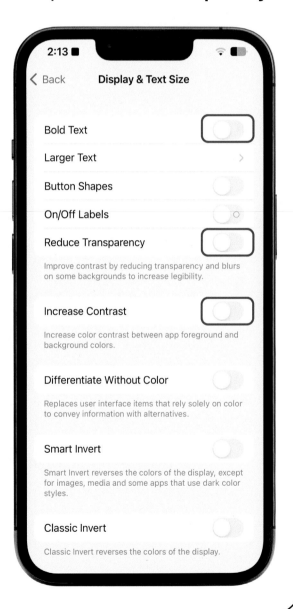

SKILL 4 How to make your phone screen brighter

Your phone's screen is able to change how bright it is depending on where you are, but sometimes the phone sets the screen brightness at the wrong level which can be frustrating. You can follow the steps below to easily change your phone screen brightness.

STEP 1. Unlock your phone and reach the homescreen as in Skill 1.

STEP 2. Place your finger on the upper right most corner of the screen. This is different from unlocking your phone or reaching the home screen because **your finger starts on the screen not off it.**

STEP 3. Swipe roughly a quarter of the way down the screen and lift up your finger. A new screen should appear. It should have many different rounded squares with different symbols in them. If you've reached a different menu, swipe up from the bottom of your screen like you did when you unlocked your phone. Now you can try again.

STEP 4. In the new menu, around halfway up your screen on the right hand side you should see two rounded rectangles of the same height. The right hand one is your phone's speaker volume, **the left hand side one is the brightness slider**. It works like a linear lightswitch dimmer. Using the pad of your finger, press and immediately drag up or down on the slider.

STEP 5. If you press the slider for a long time without dragging up or down, you will open a screen dedicated to changing just screen brightness. This isn't an issue as you can update your phone brightness here. To leave this focused view, press to the left or right of the slider.

STEP 6. Now that you've updated your screen brightness, you can return to the home screen the way you usually do by swiping up from the bottom of the screen.

You're now ready to move on to learn Skill 5

SKILL 5 How to connect to the internet

The internet is great! It can help you with everything from connecting with friends to listening to radio stations that aren't available locally. Most phones have two options to connect to the internet: cellular service or Wi-Fi. Cellular is great for when you're on the go, but can be slow—and often costly—for everyday home use. In contrast, Wi-Fi—which is a made-up word to describe wireless internet—is often faster and offers a more consistent connection to the internet.

STEP 1. Unlock your phone and navigate to the home screen.

STEP 2. Open the "**Settings**" app like you did in Skill 3.

STEP 3. In the first block, you should see a row that says "**Wi-Fi.**" Select it by pressing on it firmly and briefly.

STEP 4. A new page should open. At the top of the screen in the middle you should see the title "**Wi-F**i."

STEP 5. Near the top of your screen on the right-hand side of your screen, you should see an oval like in Skill 3. It works the same way, as an on/off switch. If the oval is green, you can move on to the next step. If it's gray, press briefly and firmly on the white dot to turn on Wi-Fi.

STEP 6. You should now see two new blocks appear. The first new block is networks you have connected to already and the second new block is new networks you have never connected to. It is also possible that if you just turned your Wi-Fi on, your phone may have automatically connected to one of these previously used networks. Any network you are connected to appears on the row below the Wi-Fi on/off switch.

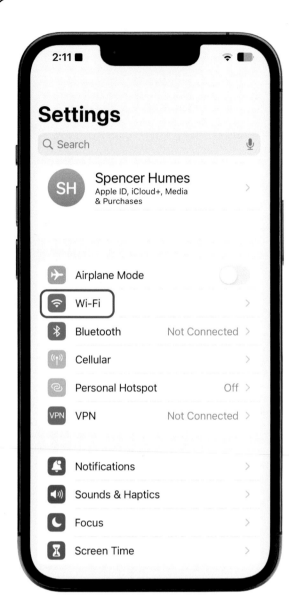

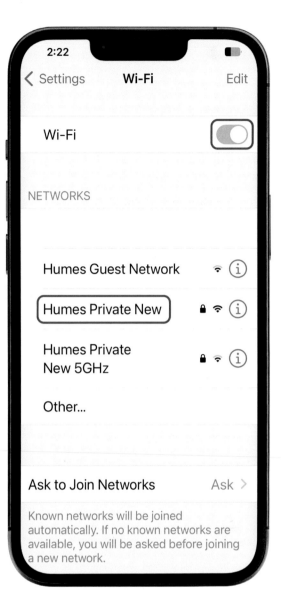

STEP 7. To choose a Wi-Fi network to connect to, press firmly and briefly on its name. Some networks have passwords. If this is the case you'll be prompted to enter one now. To do this, use the keyboard to type in the password. Be careful about capitalization. Some networks– often hotels, airports, and other large scale networks–use a sign-in portal instead of a password. These can be very different from network to network so it can be best to ask a staff member for help in connecting.

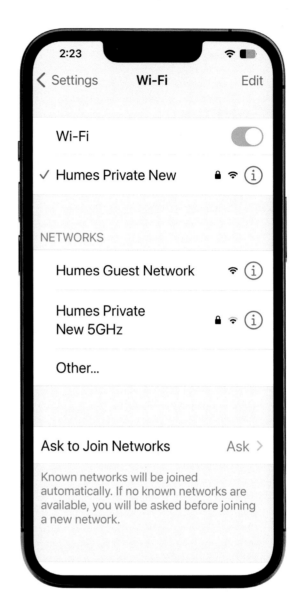

STEP 8. It's important to be careful when connecting to Wi-Fi networks in public areas. Be sure to check posted signs for the name of the official network and match it to the name of the network you're connecting to. Like with most things, if it feels risky, it is. It never hurts to be cautious and stick with cellular when you're away from any familiar networks.

You're now ready to move on to learn Skill 6

When connecting to a Wi-Fi network, remember that some networks have passwords. Use the keyboard to type in the password, being mindful of capitalization.

SKILL 6 How to navigate and read your text messages

Text messages are a great way to stay in touch. They're rarely formal and are more like writing someone a quick note than a longer letter.

STEP 1. Unlock your phone and navigate to the home screen like in Skill 1.

STEP 2. Find the "**Messages**" app and press on the icon briefly, and firmly.

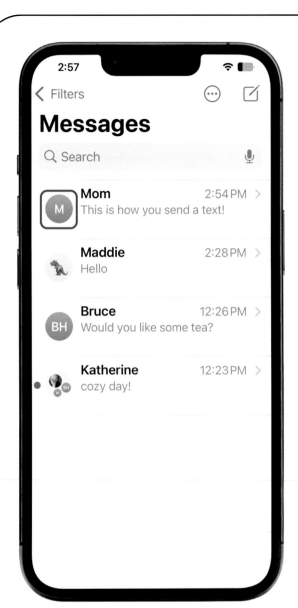

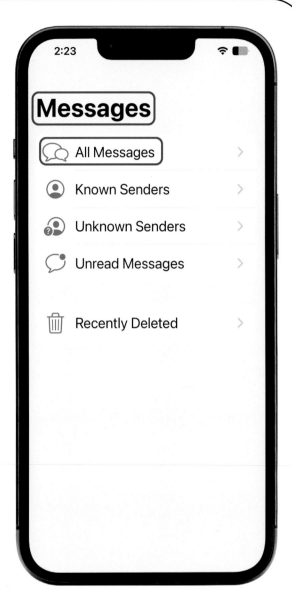

STEP 3. When the app opens, it could open a conversation, a list of conversations, or a list of different text recipients. If your app opened to a screen that says "**Messages**" near the top left and has a block of options underneath it you can move on to the next step. If not, regardless of where you are in the app, pressing the blue button in the upper left will take you back to where you need to be.

STEP 4. In the block below "**Messages**" select the first row which says "**All Messages**." This opens a list of all text conversations your phone has been a part of. If the list is empty, that just means that your phone hasn't sent or received any texts yet.

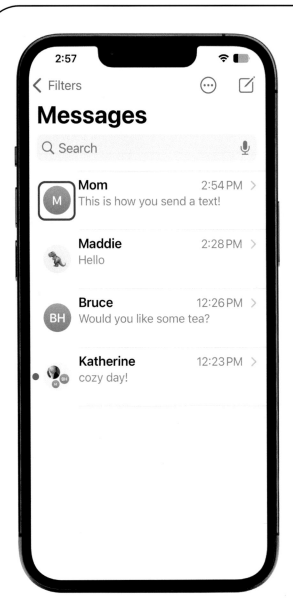

STEP 5. Each conversation is titled by the phone number, email, or name of the sender. This title is accompanied by an icon. To read a conversation, press firmly and briefly on any part of the row. It's easiest to press on the icon to make sure you select the conversation you want.

STEP 6. Once you've read the conversation—or written back as described in Skill 7—you can return to the list of all conversations by pressing the blue icon in the upper left.

You're now ready to move on to learn Skill 7

SKILL 7 How to send text messages

STEP 1. Unlock your phone and navigate to the home screen like in Skill 1.

STEP 2. Open a text conversation like in Skill 6.

STEP 3. When you open a conversation, you should see a faint gray oval box at the bottom of the screen. Press within it firmly and briefly.

STEP 4. It should move higher on the screen and a keyboard should appear beneath it.

STEP 5. Use the keyboard to compose your message. To access punctuation, press the "**123**" button in the bottom left corner. To return to the alphabet, press the "**ABC**" button in the same place. To delete one letter at a time, press the box with the x in it near the bottom right just above the "**return**" key.

STEP 6. When you're happy with your text message, press the blue arrow above your keyboard on the right hand side. When your text is delivered, it will say "**Delivered**" in faint gray letters below it.

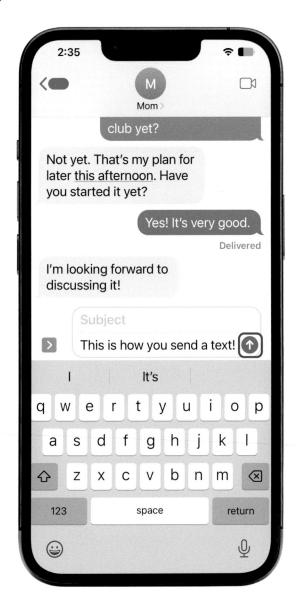

If your text does not send, a red exclamation mark will appear next to it. This is most commonly because of a slow cellular or Wi-Fi connection. When you are connected to a faster signal, press on the text and select "**Try Again**" when it appears.

You're now ready to move on to learn Skill 8

SKILL 8 How to navigate and read your email

Email is a useful tool for communicating quickly and easily with different people and organizations. It has a more formal reputation than texting and is a popular way for businesses to communicate with their customers. It aims to replace mail in some ways, but does not in other crucial areas.

AN IMPORTANT NOTE: Government organizations like the IRS will NEVER contact you by email. Similarly, banks only use email for promotions or newsletters and will use real mail to send you sensitive or important information unless you are signed up for online banking. This means that if you receive an email claiming to be from the government or a bank it should be considered fraud, especially if it contains bad news and uses urgent language. If you are concerned about the contents of the email, contact the organization it claims to represent by calling their number listed in the phone book.

STEP 1. Unlock your phone and navigate to the homescreen like in Skill 1.

STEP 2. Locate the "**Mail**" app and open it by pressing on it firmly and briefly.

STEP 3. When the app opens, it could open a specific email, a list of all emails in a particular inbox, or a list of all your inboxes. If you are on a screen titled "**Mailboxes**" with a series of blocks below it, you can move on to the next step. If not, regardless of where you are in the app, press the blue button in the top left of the screen to navigate back to where you need to be.

STEP 4. Press the first row of the first block titled "**All Inboxes.**" This will give you a list of every email on your phone that has not been archived or deleted. Each row is titled with the name of the person or organization which sent the email. Emails you haven't opened yet are marked with a blue dot. To open an email, press on its row firmly and briefly. Emails are often longer than can fit on the screen. Advance the text higher on the screen by slowly swiping up with the pad of whichever finger is most comfortable for you.

STEP 5. When you're finished reading an email, you can keep it in your inbox, archive it, or delete it.

     a. To keep an email in your inbox, press the blue button in the top left corner of your screen.

     b. To archive an email–which moves it out of your inbox and stores it for later reference–press the second button to the left on the bottom of your screen.

     c. To delete an email, press the trashcan icon, the leftmost button on the bottom of your screen.

Again, retain a healthy skepticism for any email you receive, and remember it never hurts to check in with the organization independently.

You're now ready to move on to learn Skill 9

SKILL 9 How to send an email

STEP 1. Unlock your phone and navigate to the homescreen like in Skill 1.

STEP 2. Open the "**Mail**" app like in Skill 8.

STEP 3. Navigate to the screen titled "**Mailboxes**."

STEP 4. Press the icon in the bottom right of your screen firmly and briefly. This lets you start writing a new email.

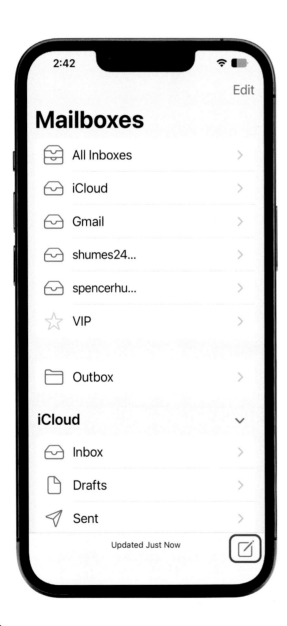

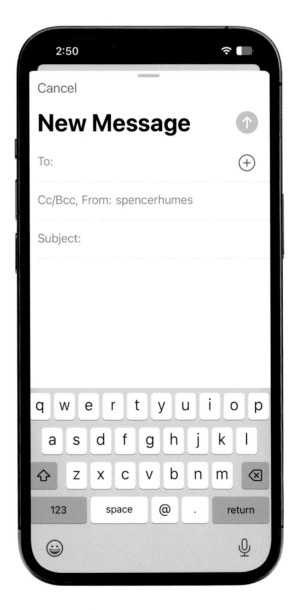

STEP 5. The first thing to do is address your email. When this screen opens, the address line is automatically selected. To make sure the address line is selected, tap once to the right of the faint gray "**To**:" at the top of the screen.

STEP 6. Use the keyboard to enter an email address. Emails follow the format "**username@provider.ext**" where a person's chosen username is separated from the name of their email provider by an "**@**". The provider's name is followed by a period and an extension like "**.com**," "**.net**," or "**.org**." This can be confusing and it can help to use an analogy to real mail.

Imagine that there are many different groups that can deliver mail—some are run by large companies, others schools, some churches, and even individuals. When you send a letter in this system, you use an email address instead of a street address. The group you use collects your mail and then delivers it to the warehouse of the group you specified after the "**@**" symbol. That group then delivers the letter to their member specified by the username before the "**@**" symbol. The three letter abbreviation at the end of the address indicates what kind of group is doing the mailing. For example, non-profit organizations use "**.org**," commercial ventures use "**.com**," educational institutions may use "**.edu**," and so on.

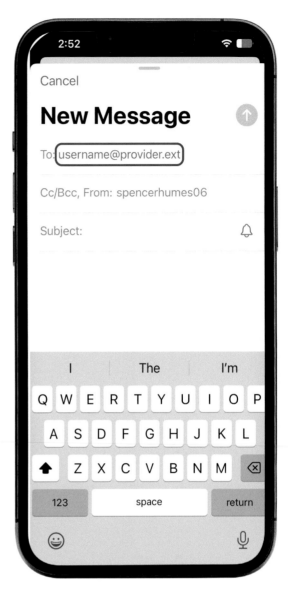

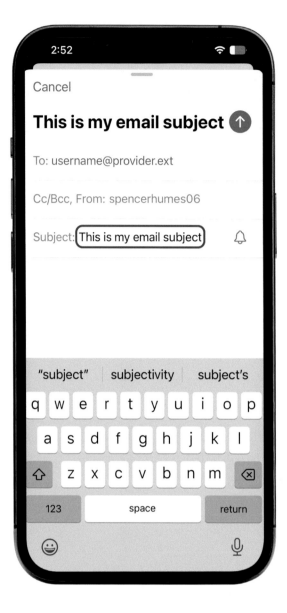

STEP 7. Once you've entered a recipient's email address, you may enter another email address separating them with a space. You can enter as many addresses as you'd like in this way. This can be useful for organizing plans with large groups.

STEP 8. To write a subject line–which serves as the title of your email–press firmly and briefly next to the faint gray text which says "**Subject**," or press the "**return**" key once. Using the keyboard, enter your desired email subject.

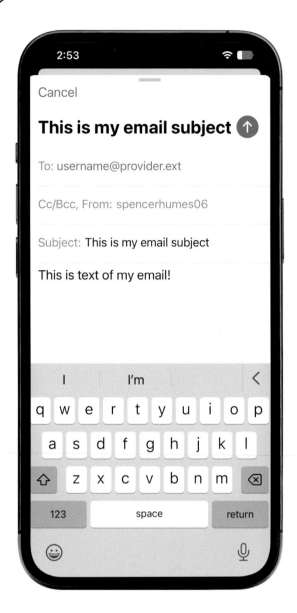
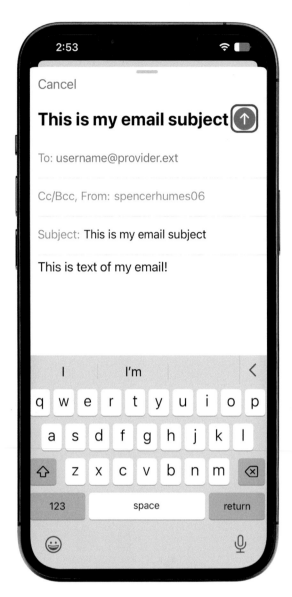

STEP 9. To write the body text of your email press firmly and briefly and the white space below your subject line, or press the "**return**" key once.

STEP 10. To send your email, press firmly and briefly on the arrow in the upper right corner. The interface will disappear, and your email will be sent. Unlike texts, if an email can't be sent due to a slow internet connection, your phone will automatically try to send it again until it is successful.

You're now ready to move on to learn Skill 10

SKILL 10 **How to call someone**

There are many ways to call someone on a smartphone, but the easiest is by dialing their number. This can be especially helpful if you have an existing rolodex or notebook of important phone numbers.

STEP 1. Unlock your phone and navigate to the homescreen like in Skill 1.

STEP 2. Open the "**Phone**" app by pressing on its icon firmly and briefly.

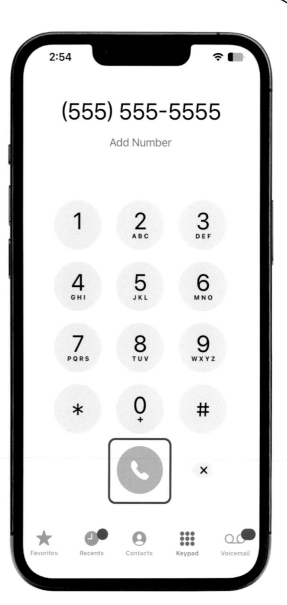

STEP 3. On the bottom of your screen, you should see five icons with faint gray text underneath them. Press the second icon from the right firmly and briefly. This opens your phone's keypad.

STEP 4. Dial your desired number by pressing each number firmly and briefly. Everything you already know about dialing with a landline applies here.

STEP 5. When you've entered the number, press the green button near the bottom of the screen firmly and briefly.

STEP 6. The earpiece speaker of your phone is located at the top of your phone and the microphone is at the bottom. This lets you hold your phone and talk into it like you would a landline.

STEP 7. To put your phone into speaker-phone mode, press the icon labeled "**Speaker**" on the screen.

STEP 8. To end your call, or hang up the phone, press the red button with the phone icon on the bottom of the screen.

CONCLUSION

Congratulations! You've mastered the last skill.
Remember, using these devices is about finding an analogy that works for you and sticking with it. Things will change, but you'll be able to figure out what to do by focusing on the 'why' behind each button.

I'd like to extend my deepest gratitude for your support of NanaTech. You make this possible.